Christmas PILGRIMS

A Journey to See Jesus

Christmas PILGRIMS

A Journey to See Jesus

Michael B. McElroy

Christmas Pilgrims—A Journey to See Jesus

Copyright © 2018 by Michael B. McElroy

Published in the United States of America by Sedgefield Press

ISBN-13: 978-0-9830655-1-7

Dedication

To my mother, Myra Nell Parker McElroy,
who taught me to read and write, to love books and
words and Christmas. But most of all, Mom, you and
Dad (Maron Byron McElroy, 1927-1990) taught me to
love and serve Jesus. I am so grateful to God
for you both.

Prologue

A conversation in Heaven...

"It is time."

"I am ready."

"The journey is a long one, as you know. The mission will be costly, to me, to you. But the objective is glorious."

"I am ready to do your will."

"It will be unpleasant there. Few will understand. Even fewer will be receptive. You will be treated shamefully."

"The only part I fear is the separation from you. I've never known that before."

"The plan will not work unless you are willing to endure it."

"I am willing."

"Then go, my Son. Go and keep our promises. Go and be who you must be and do what you must do to accomplish our purpose. I will be with you.

We will celebrate when you come home, victorious."

"I love you, Father."

"I love you, too, my Son.

November 26

*"Let us go over to Bethlehem
and see this thing that has happened,
which the Lord has made known to us."
And they went with haste and found
Mary and Joseph, and the baby
lying in a manger. - Luke 2:15-16*

They come back every year. Like the swallows returning to Capistrano on March 19, the pilgrims arrive at our house on November 1. They stay about a month. They appear with a turkey much larger than themselves. When they stand too close together, it's a scene from *A Jurassic Park Thanksgiving*. He's carrying a ceramic musket, but it's not going to be big enough to bring down that turkey. She's wearing a crisp white ceramic apron, ready to cook whatever ceramic game he brings home from the hunt. But if her pilgrim man encounters this turkeysaurus, not only will he not bring home the turkey, he won't come home at all.

Like most Americans, I associate the word *pilgrim* with the Mayflower, Plymouth Rock, Squanto and those blocky shoes with silver buckles on them. But the word pilgrim had a meaning long before those brave men and women arrived on the grassy sand dunes of Cape Cod on November 9, 1620.

They were pilgrims because of what they were doing. They were travelers on a journey with a spiritual purpose. Like Chaucer's band in *The Canterbury Tales*, like Bunyan's Pilgrim in *Pilgrim's Progress*, like the ancient Israelites who made the annual trek to appear before the Lord in Jerusalem, the pilgrims who came to America were driven by a spiritual motive.

Our American history and folklore has forever tied pilgrims to Thanksgiving. But this is a book about pilgrims of the Christmas variety—and not those pilgrims who flock to Bethlehem every December to be where Jesus was born on the traditional anniversary of his birth. Instead, I invite you to be a Christmas Pilgrim with me—to come along on a journey of the mind and heart to Bethlehem. Along the journey toward our destination, I will tell you stories about other pilgrims who made the trip, what they saw and experienced and how it changed their lives.

During the busy Christmas season, I'm sure you already have something in common with the hurrying shepherds in our text. You're probably in a hurry, too. But they weren't running late for the next holiday party or scurrying to meet the shipping deadline for Christmas Eve delivery of gifts. The shepherds weren't hurrying to the mall or to the post office. They were hurrying to Bethlehem. I'm asking you to step away from those other hurries you're in to join them for this journey. I hope you can find each day—for the next 30 days—a few moments apart from the frantic holiday pace to reflect on what the shepherds and the other pilgrims found when they arrived in little Bethlehem.

I hope you'll accept my invitation to come along on this journey. I hope you'll get a glimpse of some sacred wonders. And I hope you will be forever changed. Because I want this journey to be as personal as possible, I will call you Pilgrim along the way. I hope that is alright.

November 27

Mary and Joseph, the Magi and the shepherds were all called away from where they were and from what they were doing to come to Bethlehem for the birth of Jesus. They did not know the word *Christmas*, but they answered the call issued through soldiers, stars and angels to journey to the city of David. These original Christmas Pilgrims were forever changed by the experience.

What does it mean to you? Have you been called away from all the busyness and pressure of the Christmas season to experience the truth about the birth of Jesus? Has the fact of Jesus coming into the world changed you?

I doubt that it is possible to see and know what Jesus' birth means in a hurry or in a crowd. Our hurry-up, do more, filled-to-overflowing days are incompatible with contemplation and reflection. It is only in stillness and calm that we find truth and learn how it affects our lives.

Do you find, as I do, that the frantic pace of modern life is detrimental to your spiritual health? We are all so busy that the idea of spending daily, quiet, quality time with God just seems impossible. We all sing the same refrain: "I just do not have time." But we may need to admit to ourselves that an impossibly crowded schedule makes poor soil in which to grow a healthy, productive spiritual life.

Finding a place to be alone for a little while may also be a challenge. Some people thrive in crowds while others wilt. Whatever your reaction to being in a crowd might be, few of us are privileged to spend much time alone. The people with whom we live and work every day can be channels of blessing from God; they can also block intended blessings. A wise pilgrim knows he needs company along the way as well as some solitude.

Why is this pilgrimage a solitary one? Going to Bethlehem to look in the manger is an intensely personal matter. The fact of Jesus' birth is one thing. But the impact of that fact on your life is something more. It's not enough to know how the events at Bethlehem changed the world or even how the birth of that baby affected others. Christmas Pilgrims also need to see how they may be be personally changed by Mary's child.

November 28

Yes, Pilgrim, you and I, just like those first pilgrims, need to be "called away" for Christmas. I don't know exactly who or what might be your messenger, calling you to come. I'm pretty sure it won't be a Roman soldier, and probably neither a star nor an angel. Maybe it could be a song or a sermon. It might even be this little book. But if you hear the call, please answer it. If you really answer the call, you will be forever changed.

You need to be called away to learn about God's power, God's faithfulness and God's love. It is easy to know these matters on an intellectual level and completely miss their impact on your life. It will really help you to know in the private place of your heart what these concepts mean.

Whatever adjustments you make to your routine in order to have some time for personal contemplation will be well worth the trouble. We find the key to release us from the prison of worries, doubts and fears when we learn these lessons and apply them personally.

What better way to deal with gnawing guilt and empty loneliness than to look into the manger-cradle and see the one whose names mean "Savior" and "God with us?" Have doubt and skepticism jaded you to the point where you trust no one, not even yourself? Wouldn't it be like cleaning a smudged, dirty window to get a fresh look at the reminder in flesh that God keeps every promise?

And somewhere deep inside, don't our hearts long for the assurance that we are loved, especially when we understand how unlovable we really are? If your worship is more a stifling ritual than an exercise in genuine spiritual awareness, if your intellect is crowding out your sense of wonder, you should find this pilgrimage helpful.

Mary

November 29

*In those days a decree went out
from Caesar Augustus that all the
world should be registered.*
- Luke 2:1

The soldiers' body armor clanked as they walked into the market square at the center of the village. Their helmets and shields reflected the sun as they waited for the gathering crowd. They wore their battle gear not because they were threatened by the peasants, but as a subtle reminder of Rome's authority over her subjects.

Palestine was a remote outpost of the vast empire, and there was no glory associated with their present assignment. On this tour of the dusty towns of Galilee they were couriers, messenger boys. The ranking soldier reached into his leather pack and pulled out the scroll. He untied the thin leather strap that secured the scroll, and allowed it to unroll without much dramatic flair.

Just as he had done in the last miserable village, just as he would do in the next one, he cleared his throat and read the decree: "By decree of His Excellency Caesar Augustus, all subjects of Rome will be registered." A murmur rippled through the villagers. They knew that the census was for one purpose—to establish tax rolls. The imperial messenger continued: "Most excellent Quirinius, your benevolent governor, orders all Jewish subjects to report to their ancestral hometowns for registration."

The murmur grew into a hubbub as the words of the decree were spoken. Life was hard; how could they pay any more taxes? Travel was dangerous and difficult; how could they be expected to make the trip? A few of the more devout citizens said a silent prayer to God to send Messiah soon to rescue them from the oppressors.

Mary was returning from the market stalls with food for the day when she heard the announcement. Her progressing pregnancy made walking more difficult. Now just a few months from the baby's arrival came word that she and Joseph would have to travel 90 miles to Judea, to Bethlehem for the tax census. Her neighbors were complaining, and she understood their frustration. She held the food basket in one hand and instinctively cradled her growing belly with her other arm as she felt the baby moving inside her. But she had a quiet smile on her face as she realized how God was going to get her to the place where Micah had predicted hundreds of years before that her baby would be born.

Pilgrim, can you think of a way that God might be at work in some unpleasant circumstance you're facing right now? Can you trust that he is working in it even if you can't see how? Ask God to give you a faith like Mary had.

November 30

"Behold, I am the servant of the
Lord; let it be to me according to
your word." - Luke 1:38

Our perspective about this journey to Bethlehem depends on what we know about our purpose for going there. To the soldiers who announced the travel plans to the residents of Nazareth, it was a matter of duty. It was their duty to deliver the orders, and it was the duty of Rome's subjects to obey.

Have you ever obeyed out of duty? Have you completed a task or complied with a directive without any sense of joy or privilege because it was simply a matter of duty? I am ashamed to admit that I have done some good things that I hope were a blessing to other people in some circumstances where I had little or no joy in the task. Just as we pity those who deceive themselves, so we may pity ourselves and others who rob themselves of blessings by only doing spiritual work out of duty.

Pilgrim, I hope you're beginning this journey to Bethlehem with hopeful expectation, not hopeless resignation. I cannot come through the page, twist your arm and compel you to come along. I can only invite you to come, promise you that it will be worth the trip and thank you for the time you're investing. You could miss the point if the daily reading and pondering become burdensome duties in your mind so, please, don't let that happen.

I want to kindle (or perhaps rekindle) your sense of awe and appreciation for what we're going to see in Bethlehem. The wonder and worship I want you to experience will be incompatible with resentment about having to go along. Like a child forced to visit relatives when the child would rather stay home and play, we sometimes pout and miss some really fine experiences when our attitude is negative.

I doubt there was much joy in the villages and towns of Galilee and Judea as the news of the census spread. But I imagine one heart heard and received a very different message from the announcement. Mary's life had been interesting in the past few months, to say the least. She was young, engaged and her whole life was before her when the angel appeared and told her she was going to have a baby. She was innocent, but knew enough to know that she could not possibly be pregnant. As the angel explained how it was going to happen, she humbly accepted the plan and her place in it. "Behold, I am the servant of the Lord; let it be to me according to your word." That spirit of submission to God's will, Pilgrim, is the key to the rest of her story—and ours.

How would you describe the difference in how it feels to submit because of trust rather than obey out of duty? Which has been more characteristic of your relationship with God so far?

December 1

*"Behold, I am the servant of the
Lord; let it be to me according to
your word." - Luke 1:38*

Would you focus with me one more day on Mary's words? What an amazing display of unconditional, servant-hearted surrender! I admit that some of my "surrendering" has not always been unconditional. How about you? Have you ever had that sense of complete surrender about your life and God's will for it?

I'm pretty sure we rob ourselves of a blessing when we insert exceptions and escape clauses in our surrender to the Lord. I imagine, like me, Pilgrim, you have done that - even though we know that genuine surrender relieves much stress and frustration about obedience. When we are willing for God's plan, whatever it is, to guide our lives and take us where he wants us to go, we are blessed with peace that can withstand every difficult circumstance and overcome every obstacle.

That doesn't mean there won't be any difficult circumstances or obstacles. I do not imagine Mary's life was easy in the aftermath of the angel's announcement. Think of having to tell Joseph.

"Honey, I'm going to have a baby."

"Yes, dear, if the Lord blesses us with a child, we will be so happy. I can hardly wait."

"No, you don't understand. I am pregnant. Right now. I am going to have a baby."

"But that's impossible!" And then Joseph's face was a kaleidoscope of emotion as incredulity turned to doubt, doubt turned to suspicion, suspicion turned to hurt, and hurt turned into anger.

"Let me explain! An angel came and talked to me. He told me I was going to have a baby! And the baby is the Son of God!" For all the times she had rehearsed it, the story was still hard to believe. (Reality check: If you were a father, would you believe your daughter if she told you such a story? If you were a mother, would you take your daughter's word for it? If you were engaged, would you expect your fiancé to believe a story like that?) We know this story from Sunday School. It's in the Bible. But when Mary had to tell Joseph, they weren't in Sunday School and it wasn't in the Bible (yet). Had the angel not also appeared to Joseph and verified her story, Mary would have been divorced before she was ever married.

If it ever seems to you that God's will is demanding and difficult, consider the self-sacrificing spirit that Mary showed as the events unfolded that would send her on pilgrimage to Bethlehem. And marvel at her amazing surrender.

Has following God's will ever created friction in one of your relationships? How does surrender relieve the tension you may feel about making a big decision?

December 2

*"You are blessed, because you
believed the Lord would do
what he said." - Luke 1:45, NLT*

Mary couldn't wait to head for the hills. She had to see Elizabeth. Her old relative's round belly would be tangible evidence that what the angel said was true. When she saw that Elizabeth was pregnant, just as the angel said, she could make more sense of what the angel had told her about her own pregnancy.

When she arrived in the little town in the Judean hill country where Zechariah and Elizabeth lived, she went to their house and called out to Elizabeth. Dr. Luke tells us that the baby in Elizabeth's womb leaped within her at the sound of Mary's voice and that Elizabeth was filled with the Holy Spirit. The reference to the Spirit explains how this old woman, mysteriously pregnant herself, became the first human in the story to call Mary's baby "Lord." She told her young visitor how honored she was that the mother of her Lord had come to see her, and about the baby within her jumping for joy when Mary spoke.

All of this confirmed for Mary what the angel had said a few days before. Had Mary, at this stage, told anyone else about the angel's message? Had she wondered how she would explain it, and who in their right mind would believe it? And then, before she even got to tell her, Elizabeth knew all about it and was celebrating!

Elizabeth said an interesting thing to Mary about the young woman's blessedness. She said, "You are blessed, because you believed that the Lord would do what he said." That line is a great one for Christmas Pilgrims like you and me to embrace. It embodies the whole journey of Abraham and his descendants through the pages of the Old Testament. It summarizes the good news of the gospel, explaining in the simplest terms why and how God's scheme of redemption can work. It explains how thousands who responded to the good news in Acts were saved. It's the basis for the changed lives and new hope of those disciples addressed in letters we now call the epistles in the New Testament.

Pilgrim, it's important for you to understand how this statement applies to us on our own journeys. It's about believing that God did what he said he would do about the baby in Mary's womb being the Son of God. But we also need to believe that God will do what he has promised in our own lives.

Recall a time when you trusted God's promise and were blessed by doing so. Give thanks!

Can you think of any promise God has made that you need to trust more to enjoy a blessing he wants to give you?

December 3

*"You are blessed, because you
believed the Lord would do what he
said." - Luke 1:45, NLT*

Let's linger another day on this verse that so
beautifully shows the relationship between trusting
God's word and being blessed by him.

I wrote a little devotional book for our church family
a few years ago that consisted of fifty promises from
Scripture and an application to our lives. With a few
volunteers, we printed and bound it right there in the
church offices. We read it together in a fifty-day period
to strengthen our faith. From the promise of salvation
inherent in Jesus' name to the promise that God would
be our Father to the promise that he would be at work in,
on and through us, we listened and meditated on what
God said he would do. He will provide for you; he will
give you wisdom; he will never forsake you. He will
guard your heart, grant you rest and give you eternal life.
The list goes on and on. And though in that little book I
did not refer to today's text, every day we came to realize
a little more of what Elizabeth meant: We really are
blessed when we believe that the Lord will do what he
has said.

Pilgrim, believe me, it is true—we get blessed when
we trust God. That blessing may come in the form of joy
over the worst problem in our lives being solved. That
blessing may be the peace we find when we pray instead
of worry. Or it may come in the form of confidence to

face whatever comes because we know that he is with us, and like David said so long ago, "I will fear no evil, for you are with me."

Christmas Pilgrims can bank on this: when we study the promises of God, reflect on what those promises mean to us, and embrace them in trusting faith, God will bless us! Then we realize with joy that we are heirs of the promises God made long ago to Abraham. God is trustworthy; God does not lie. Pilgrim, you won't be disappointed or let down when you believe what he tells you. You will, along with Mary, be blessed because you believe.

Why is it sometimes difficult to trust a promise? Can you think of a promise from God that has been especially meaningful to you?

December 4

"My soul magnifies the Lord, and
my spirit rejoices in God my Savior."
- Luke 1:46-47

Some religions hold out hope to humans that they can somehow become God. But Christianity revolves around the idea that God became one of us in the person of Jesus. The mystery of the Incarnation is focused most sharply in the events surrounding the birth of Jesus.

We who believe the gospel accept by faith that God caused a baby to grow within Mary's womb without a human father. Believing in God as the Creator of our world paves the way for believing that he could cause a virgin to bear a child. If God made the original human beings as Genesis says he did, causing a baby to grow in a woman's body without a human father should be far easier, not impossibly difficult. Still, we can sympathize with Mary, who asked, "How can this be?" And the angel's answer to her should satisfy us as well: "For nothing will be impossible with God."

The Magnificat, or Mary's song, is a sublime expression of praise and devotion to God. It is steeped in Scripture. Mary knew the prophecies and believed the promises. As she saw what God was doing in her own life, as her awareness of his plan and her place in it grew, her sense of wonder and adoration overflowed in worshipful praise.

Seeing baby Jesus in Bethlehem should fill you and me with awe and praise, too. Our minds reel at the paradox of the Creator lying on a bed of straw, wrapped in cloth. The one who by his power created the plants that produced his bed and bedclothes now lies helpless in the manger. Like those confusing images of reflections of reflections in parallel mirrors, it is staggering to contemplate a mother giving birth to a baby who gave her life. Faith accepts what it cannot figure out; it takes over when understanding fails.

The baby in the manger reminds us of how far God was willing to go to get us back. When sin entered the world and the whole human family became alienated from their maker by sin, God demonstrated his love for us by sending Jesus to die for us. To die for us, he had to live among us and be flesh and blood like us.

We know that trust is not tested until we want something different from what God has commanded, or when we can't understand why. Can you think of an example of these "trust tests" in your own life?

December 5

*And Mary said to the angel, "How
will this be, since I am a virgin?"*
- Luke 1:34

After the angel explained it to him, Joseph accepted
Mary's incredible news and went ahead with the
wedding, denying himself the pleasure and privilege of
being with his wife until after the baby was born. But
Joseph's was not the only judgment Mary had to face. In
the little town of Nazareth, the family and neighbors
soon knew. Mary had to accept the burden of public
opinion as the baby grew within her womb. I doubt that
people were much different then than they are now. The
whispered gossip probably made it unpleasant to go to
the market or to the synagogue.

Yet despite the hardship, Mary was willing. She
recognized the Roman decree as the means by which
God's promises to Abraham, David and Mary would be
kept, and the intricate prophetic detail of Messiah being
born in Bethlehem would be fulfilled. If nobody else in
town liked the orders, if every one of her neighbors
resented the census, Mary knew and understood God's
purpose in sending her to Bethlehem.

Knowing that God has a purpose for our lives is
fundamental to a genuine walk with him. Do you trust
that his hand is on the circumstances of your life-journey,
even the unpleasant, difficult ones? Mary must have
known this as she was faithful through a difficult season
of life that was neither by her choice nor under her

control. When we believe God is sovereign, we can accept the fact that he can use the events and situations of our lives, even those we bring upon ourselves by our own choices, to accomplish his purpose.

The apostle Paul said, "We walk by faith, not by sight." Do you filter news and turns of events through your trusting faith that God knows, sees and loves you? Do you trust that he wants what is best for you? Many counselors and philosophers have noted that we cannot control the circumstances of life, but we can control our response to those circumstances. This should ring most true to people of faith. When we worry about what will happen, what people will think and how we will ever make it, that anxiety is a warning light on the dashboard of life. If I'm worried, I'm probably running low on faith.

As Christmas Pilgrims, on our way to Bethlehem, I hope we will rely more and more upon a God who is absolutely reliable. Like Mary, I hope we can see the hand of God at work, even in the actions of people around us who may deny God or be indifferent to him. And like the young woman chosen to be the mother of our Lord, I hope that our hearts will be devoted and our wills submitted to his purpose and plans.

Recall a time when you felt anxious because you did not know what was going to happen. How is trust different from knowledge?

Joseph

December 6

And Joseph also went up from
Galilee, from the town of Nazareth, to
Judea, to the city of David, which is
called Bethlehem, because he was of
the house and lineage of David, to be
registered with Mary, his betrothed,
who was with child. - Luke 2:4-5

Joseph had a life before he was a Bethlehem-bound pilgrim. He was already established in the village of Nazareth. He had a family history, too. Today we struggle to establish our family's genealogy beyond three or four generations. But in that primitive time before searchable online records and genealogy software, Joseph and his relatives knew they were descended from Judah's greatest descendent, David. Of course this heritage ties him to our story and pilgrimage as he is on his way to Bethlehem precisely because he is from that tribe, clan and family.

The verses here also suggest Joseph's future. Not only did the quiet carpenter have a past, he had a plan for the future, too. He was committed to spending the rest of his life with the woman at his side, Mary. They were betrothed. More than engaged, Joseph and Mary were legally pledged to be married. The plans and dreams of a young couple stretched out before them. They were past the shock of the news about Mary's pregnancy. They would make the journey to Bethlehem to comply with the Roman's decree. The baby would be born, and they would get on with their life together. But the journey to Bethlehem and what would happen there would shape and define the rest of their lives.

These verses remind us that our own pilgrim journey fits into the context of a life. If the journey is our present, we, like Joseph have a past, a history. We all join this pilgrim band with what the novelist calls a backstory—events that shaped us and brought us to the present time. And don't we all have hopes and dreams for the future as well? How will making this journey to Bethlehem change us?

Jesus came to Bethlehem to deal with our past. We've all said and done things we're not very happy to recall. Embarrassment and shame well up inside us as we contemplate mistakes we made that hurt not only us, but others around us as well. Guilt gnaws at those who have done their best over wrongs that left scars on their gentle conscience. For all those reasons and more, the Savior came to be born so he could die to take away the guilt.

Jesus came to Bethlehem to give us a future with hopes and dreams instead of fear and dread. No one who makes this journey has to go away hopeless. There's not one Christmas Pilgrim who comes to the manger who must go away with the pain of emptiness and the frustration of brokenness. We find strength to face whatever the future holds when we trust the promises made and sealed by the one who was born at Bethlehem. We can reshape our perspective on life by learning how precious we are to the Father who sent his Son. As we go from Bethlehem, heeding his words and walking in his footsteps, our futures are dramatically different.

It's very important for pilgrims to know that the journey of the here and now cannot be separated from the history that precedes it and the legacy that will follow it. Without Jesus, that sounds like a curse. Apart from his power to redeem and change us, we'd be no more than helpless victims of our personal choices and impersonal fate. But Jesus offers a release from the ugly past, and promises the resources of heaven itself to secure our future.

We need not allow anxiety about yesterday or tomorrow to rob us of today. Stories about time travel are probably popular because we sense how truly confined we are in the present. Who hasn't entertained the idea of going back to change some decision that altered the course of life? Every daydreamer is imagining how it will be in the future. But the baby born at Bethlehem is the only one who can really do anything about either past or future.

Do you struggle with memories or guilt about the past? How can Jesus help with that?

Are you anxious about the future? How can strong trusting faith in God overcome our worries?

December 7

"Is not this the carpenter's son?"
- Matthew 13:55

Like the wise men, Joseph is cloaked in mystery. Like the shepherds, an angel told him where to go and what to do. From the genealogy, we know the names of his father and ancestors. We know he was a carpenter (literally *tekton*, perhaps stone mason). The Bible tells us no word that he spoke. We do not know how or when he died, but we presume that he died before Jesus began his public ministry.

It's odd, yet appropriate that we know so little about this fellow God chose to be the father figure in Jesus' life. You'd think we'd have more information about such an important character in the story. But since he wasn't really Jesus' father, the gospel writers' lack of detail about him almost seems to verify the fact that he's really in the background of this story.

I do think Joseph must have been involved in Jesus' training and development as a young child. Joseph surely must have taught Jesus his trade. That must have been a little ironic, too. What's a carpenter going to teach the Creator of the universe about building something? And from what little we know about Mary's husband, I'm sure that Jesus saw a good example of self-denial and godliness in Joseph.

Like another Joseph, the one from the book of Genesis, this Joseph was a dreamer. On three occasions, an angel of the Lord appeared to the Joseph in our story via a dream, telling him to marry Mary, to flee to Egypt and to return to the land of Israel after Herod's death. In a dream, an angel convinced Joseph that Mary's baby was the Son of God, not the son of some other man. Each time, Joseph got up and did what the angel of the Lord told him to do.

I don't know a lot about dreams. About the only kind I can ever remember are the ones that I don't want to come true! But I do know that God used dreams in the past to communicate. That's another of those "various ways" God has chosen to speak through the ages.

How many generations of your family do you remember or know about? Parents? Grandparents? Great-grandparents? Who in your family shaped your early life and values?

December 8

And when the time came for their
purification according to the Law of
Moses, they brought him up to
Jerusalem to present him to the Lord.
- Luke 2:22

Perhaps the best lesson we Christmas Pilgrims can take from this quiet, mysterious man is to listen to God and do what he says. It's tempting to say, "If the Lord spoke to me in a dream, I'd do whatever God said." Maybe so. But are we listening and doing what he has already told us?

Joseph listened to God and followed instructions that came through more ordinary channels, too. Luke says the trips to Jerusalem for Jesus' circumcision and later for his presentation as the firstborn at the temple were "according to the law of Moses" and "as it is written in the Law of the Lord." Joseph and Mary knew what God's word said, and they were doing it.

Let's not dismiss all teaching about obedience as "legalistic." Legalism is not about knowing and doing God's will. Legalism is trusting law-keeping as the basis of righteousness. It binds human opinion and dogma as if man-made rules were the very words of God.

Joseph's trust in God shines in his humble obedience. I wish my life had more consistently demonstrated my trust. Pilgrim, I wonder, do you feel the same way about yourself?

Jesus said, "If you love me, you will obey what I command." Have you ever been hurt by someone who claimed to love you, but showed no consideration for you in their actions? Love is not just professed; Paul described how love behaves (not how it feels) in 1 Corinthians 13. Love is lived out every day in what we do. If we love ourselves more than we love Jesus, it shows. When we love the world, or sinful pleasure or the acceptance of other people more than we love God, it shows in our choices, conduct and character.

Are we really disciples of Jesus if we do not heed his words and follow his steps? The purpose of learning from Jesus and following him is to become like him, to reflect his will and heart in our own lives. John wrote, "We know that we have come to know him if we obey his commands," and, "Whoever claims to live in him must walk as Jesus did." Paul said he had been crucified with Christ—that he no longer lived, but Christ lived in him. He was doing what Jesus called disciples to do— deny self, take up the cross daily and follow him.

From the little we know about Joseph's life, it's clear that he was obedient. That obedience led him on his pilgrimage to Bethlehem. If we really want to see and know the Lord, we will obey him, too. Obedience will not be a prideful badge of how good we are, or a measuring stick to judge fellow pilgrims. But we can know the joy of showing our faith in Jesus and our love for him by doing what he tells us to do.

Why do you think obedience is closely tied to both faith and love in the Bible?

Is all obedience or teaching about obedience "legalism?" Why or why not?

December 9

*When Joseph woke from sleep, he
did as the angel of the Lord
commanded him: he took his wife, but
knew her not until she had given birth
to a son. And he called his name
Jesus. - Matthew 1:24-25*

The few words we read about Joseph in the gospel reveal another dimension of his selflessness. I realize that selfishness lies at the root of what I do that displeases God. Have you noticed that about yourself, Pilgrim? How many of the crimes, abuses, wars and other daily news items are rooted in selfishness?

Matthew says Joseph took Mary home as his wife after the angel told him about the baby, but he had no union with her until she gave birth to Jesus. Later in the story, when Jesus grew up and began his ministry, the people of his hometown were amazed by him and asked, "Isn't this the carpenter's son? Isn't his mother's name Mary? Aren't his brothers and sisters here with us?" That indicates that Joseph and Mary did have a normal life as husband and wife after Jesus was born. But before the birth of Jesus, Joseph did not experience the pleasure of being with Mary, though he was legally married to her.

Popular culture would have us believe that sex is just like air or water—you can't live long without it. Some folks say it's unreasonable to expect young people to abstain from sexual relations until they are married. A single man or woman who chooses to remain single and chaste may be the object of gossip and suspicion. Some married people have used their spouse's inability to have sex due to pregnancy or some illness as an excuse to break their vows.

In contrast to all that, Joseph denied himself the privilege of union with his wife until after Jesus was born. It was a selfless thing to do.

Christmas is a time when we show our selflessness or our selfishness. Do you remember litmus paper from science lab? It reveals whether a substance is an acid or a base by changing color on contact with the substance. Maybe the pretty wrapping paper on presents under our Christmas trees works like litmus paper. Are we more excited about the gifts we receive and unwrap, or the ones we wrap and give? The way we give and receive may reveal our hearts to be either selfless or selfish.

It's normal for kids to be excited about what they're going to "get" for Christmas. As we become parents and grandparents, we tend to get more excited about what we're giving than getting. It is thrilling to watch a child grow in the grace of giving and learn that Jesus was right (he always is) when he said, "It is more blessed to give than to receive."

Can you recall a gift you were more excited about giving than receiving? To whom did you give it, and why was it so rewarding to give?

Who has been an example of selfless love in your life? What could you do today to imitate their good example?

The Angels

December 10

And the angel said to them, "Fear not, for behold, I bring you good news of great joy that will be for all the people." - Luke 2:10

How far did the angels travel to make the announcement to the shepherds that night? How long did it take them to reach the field where the shepherds were watching their flocks? How were the spokesangel and the choir selected from heaven's host?

I don't know as much about the angels as I'd like to know. Once when I was the guest speaker at a church, a woman asked me how much I knew about angels. I told her I didn't know very much. The next night she brought me a copy of her book about angels along with a bill for it.

I suspect that real angels aren't very much like the little ceramic ones on the shelves in the gift shops. The shepherds probably wouldn't have been terrified if a host of little cherubs appeared and strummed out a birth announcement on their tiny harps.

Glimpses we get of real angels in the Bible suggest they are strong and fast. They are warriors. They are hit men. They are saviors and guides to their human charges. And they are messengers. The etymology of the word *angel* is tied up in bearing a message.

On our pilgrimage to Bethlehem, I want to probe deeper into what the angels said to the shepherds. I think a closer look at the familiar words from Luke 2 will help us on our way.

First, the angel said, "Don't be afraid." That's pretty much the standard opening line for angels in encounters with people, especially people who are getting good news from God through their angelic messenger. This tells me a couple of things.

It backs up my earlier suggestion that real angels are much bigger and scarier than the ones commonly depicted on coffee mugs and calendars. These celestial beings from beyond this world may disguise themselves as ordinary people. (How else could Abraham or we entertain angels without knowing it?) But I suspect shock and awe is probably the normal human reaction to a close encounter with an angel.

It's good to know the word of God from these mighty messengers was not a threat, but an announcement of good news. The character and nature of God and his divine purposes for us are good and positive. A respectful fear of the Lord that leads us to listen and obey is not the same thing as the terror that comes to those who rebel against God and defy his authority over their lives. As a race, we certainly deserve to be terrified when God or one of his messengers arrives on the scene, but the keynote of most angelic announcements is "Fear not."

Has fear ever been your first reaction to something different or unfamiliar? Have you ever feared something that turned out to be good instead of bad?

December 11

And the angel said to them, "Fear not, for behold, I bring you good news of great joy that will be for all the people." - Luke 2:10

The next thing the angel said was, "I bring you good news of great joy!" Some days when we watch or read or listen to the news, it seems that *good* and *news* don't fit very well together. There's a war here, a threat to your health there. The terror alert has been elevated, a fire is burning out of control, a once-admired public figure has disgraced himself in a scandal. When the announcer says, "We'll have more news after this message," it almost seems like a threat.

But the angel had good news that was going to bring great joy. In announcing the birth of the Savior, the winged correspondent was telling his audience their worst problem was going to be solved, and their worst fears would be allayed. The long-predicted, long-awaited one had come. I doubt the shepherds were theologically grounded enough to grasp the full meaning of the announcement. (I doubt that you or I can grasp the full meaning ourselves.) But the angel communicated the message in a way that the shepherds got the point, and the point was good, not bad news.

And the result of hearing the news was great joy. The shepherds' first reaction was terror, but it turned to joy when they listened, acted on what they heard and found the words to be true. Their joyful songs of praise to God rang out through the night as they returned to their flocks in the fields.

Is overflowing joy our reaction to messages we hear from God's word? Some folks are sad instead of joyful when they read or hear God's word. They hear the condemnation of lostness and miss the message about the Savior. This might happen because guilt has conditioned them to hear only the negative side of the news about their relationship and standing with God. Maybe pride rejects the possibility that a Savior is needed, and takes offense at the suggestion that one has been provided. It could also be the result of external factors, such as prolonged exposure to preaching that condemns by content and tone, and lacks the quality of hope-inspiring good news. Such teaching drains the hearers of joy, leaving them with a dry husk of hopelessness.

I'm not an angel, but I am a preacher. I probably need to go for a walk in the woods or down a lonely beach somewhere and think about this for a while. Does the word from God that I'm called to deliver come across as good news? Is there any evidence of joy in my hearers' hearts? I heard an old preacher say that the finest steak would be rejected if it was offered in a filthy wrapper. It is possible (perhaps even common) to deliver the best news of the gospel in distasteful words, hateful attitudes and inept teaching methods. When people hear or read it wrapped like that, they miss the good news and are robbed of the intended joy.

The news of a Savior implies the fact of sin and lostness. I do not suggest ignoring the problem of sin. Part of faithful preaching involves rebuke and convicting people of sin in their lives. But as a preacher, I must take care to tell the rest of the story. Jesus came to earth, lived a perfect life and died to pay for those sins. God's power raised him from the dead, and that same power is offered to us for living.

When we Christmas Pilgrims try to share a message from God with a friend or neighbor, let's remember these things. Let's give them hope. Let's show them how it can be better and different for them because of the good news of great joy.

Think of a time when you received some good news. What made it good? How were you affected by hearing it?

December 12

*And the angel said to them, "Fear
not, for behold, I bring you good
news of great joy that will be for all
the people." - Luke 2:10*

The angel said that the joyful good news was for all
the people. That makes this message quite different from
other kinds of news. News of rising interest is great for
investors, but not so great for borrowers. The rainy
forecast is good news for farmers and their thirsty fields,
but bad news for the folks planning a big outdoor event
at the same time. Even the sports page brings joy to the
fans on the winning side and disappointment to those
who wear the colors of the losing team.

But this announcement brought good news for
everybody. Everybody needs a Savior. This Savior has
come. The message of his saving work is addressed to all
nations and every person. And everyone can be blessed
by it! The only ones who fail to be blessed are those who
reject and refuse God's offer of salvation.

It's thrilling to think about the universal nature of the
gospel's offer. But as a Christmas Pilgrim, I need to see
myself in the picture. So do you. This news from the
angels isn't just about the Savior of the world being born.
It's first and most about *your* Savior being born. Like the
angel said, "A Savior has been born *to you* this day." I'm
not talking about the original word in the text being
singular or plural. Pilgrim, I'm asking you to take it

personally, to believe that this universal good news is addressed specifically to you.

I get mail every day that has been addressed by a machine. A computer's database associated my name and address with the bill or catalog. A mechanical device printed it on the envelope or label. The first personal human touch may have been a local postal worker who sorted it into my mail. But sometimes I get an envelope that is hand addressed. Someone took pen in hand and addressed me personally, specifically. That's the rare kind of mail I open first.

The email equivalent of this is a filter that sends email from your family, friends and associates to your Inbox. You are going to look at those emails. The rest go to Spam and may never be read at all.

The gospel is a special kind of universal. It's for everybody, but its joy-producing, life-changing good news is personally addressed to you. Don't get lost in the crowd, or think you don't fit in. Don't protest, "You don't know what I've done, or what's been done to me." You're right, I don't. But God does. And he sent Jesus to be your personal Savior. So when you make the pilgrimage to Bethlehem and look into the manger, realize that the incredible gift is for you.

What do you do with mail addressed to Box Holder or Occupant? How do you handle correspondence from a friend, or a check or a bill that comes to the same mailbox? What makes the difference?

The
Shepherds

December 13

And in the same region there were
shepherds out in the field, keeping
watch over their flock by night.
- Luke 2:8

It was an adventure for the young ones, a campout. But the older men knew it was hard work punctuated by restless bouts of trying to sleep on hard ground. It was only necessary to sleep outside a couple of times a year, although it was not uncommon for the shepherds to do so. When the ewes were bearing their young and when the overflow numbers of sheep were brought in for Passover, there was no question about where the shepherds in the suburbs of Jerusalem would spend their evenings.

There were certain perks to being outdoors, alone and away from town. The spectacle of the stars was breathtaking on cloudless nights when the air was still and cold. Brighter than diamonds on black velvet, the stars sparkled in their constellations. Even the children could recognize and name the best-known features of the night sky. And there were those rare, serene days when the temperature was not extreme, the predators were not attacking and there was sufficient pasture for the sheep to graze contentedly.

The irony of the shepherd's life was (again) the topic around the fire in an open field near Bethlehem on this night. "They need us," sneered one young man, "but they don't want us around."

It was true. A sizable portion of the local economy depended on the work of the shepherds. Yet the lowliest workers in the village looked down on shepherds as unclean and undesirable, dishonest and disenfranchised. Shepherds were not considered fit to testify in the legal proceedings conducted in the city's gate. They were outcasts, excluded from the mainstream of the culture by reason of their occupation.

How very like God to send the angels to deliver the best news Jewish society or the world could ever hear to a bunch of outcast shepherds. "Unto you is born this day, in the city of David a Savior, who is Christ the Lord." It was the ostracized who were invited to find and adore the newborn Messiah.

After the terror subsided, the shepherds hurried to Bethlehem, answering the call of the angels to come see the little King. After they found Joseph, Mary and baby Jesus, they told everyone they met about the incredible events of the night. Everyone wondered at the testimony of these shepherds who were not counted fit to testify. When the shepherds answered the call to become Christmas Pilgrims, they were changed by the things they saw and heard. True, they were still shepherds. They had to go back to the flocks and do their lowly work. Their status in society had not changed. But as the shepherds returned to their flocks in the field, their hearts were filled with joy and worship. As Mary had put it, God had looked with favor on the humble estate of his servants.

Let's remember that the angels did not appear in Herod's throne room, or in the temple courts. They went to outcasts in a field doing a job that segregated them from respectable company. Despised by their society, they were esteemed by God. The shepherds' story should give Christmas Pilgrims like you and me hope, no matter how lowly our position in life may be.

Pilgrim, have you ever felt like an outsider, like you weren't welcome or didn't fit in? What important lesson about God can we learn from the story of the shepherds?

December 14

When the angels went away from them into heaven, the shepherds said to one another, "Let us go over to Bethlehem and see this thing that has happened, which the Lord has made known to us." And they went with haste and found Mary and Joseph, and the baby lying in a manger. And when they saw it, they made known the saying that had been told them concerning this child. And all who heard it wondered at what the shepherds told them. - Luke 2:15-18

There is much we may learn from these pilgrims who smelled like sheep. People who hear good news should do something about it. They hurried to Bethlehem to see for themselves what the angels had told them. They followed the directions about how to find Jesus, Mary and Joseph. They went to see for themselves. After they came and saw, they went and told.

Beyond the personal responsibility to be aware of God and worship him, followers of Christ have the responsibility to communicate the good news in a way that captures the attention of others. The people who heard the shepherds' report were amazed by what the shepherds said. I suspect the shepherds' wide-eyed enthusiasm had something to do with the wonder their report created in their hearers.

When church is boring, it may be that we're not doing a very good job of connecting with the target audience. We may be okay with how we tell it because it's comfortably familiar to us. But we may need to think about how we present the message to our culture. Are we really "going" with the gospel? Are we imitating Paul, who said he became all things to all people to save some souls? And as we go and as we tell, do we have the shepherds' contagious, enthusiastic joy about our story?

Many people who saw and heard Jesus in person rejected him. The same will probably be true when we share the good news today. But that does not negate our responsibility to obey Jesus' orders to tell everyone about him. The sower in Jesus' story didn't get any results in some of the ground where the seed fell. But some of it did fall on the right kind of ground and produce the crop. Our joy and God's glory will be multiplied when we do what these shepherds did, and when people around us hear it and are blessed by the good news.

Do you remember who told you the good news about Jesus? What impressed you about them and their story?

Have you ever recommended a restaurant or a movie you enjoyed? Why do you think I asked you about that?

December 15

And the shepherds returned,
glorifying and praising God for all
they had heard and seen, as it had
been told them. - Luke 2:20

The news about the baby's birth came to people much like those who would receive him when he grew up and began his ministry. The orthodox would reject Jesus, but the outcasts would hear him gladly. The priests would snub, mock and accuse the Galilean, but the common people would gladly listen to him.

The angels said the good news was for all the people. Pilgrim, that would include you and me. A Savior, they said, had been born. In whatever hopeless and beaten place this news finds you, it should make a difference for you. The worst problem any of us face is the common problem we all face—our sins have separated us from God. We're lost and we need a Savior to do for us what we could never do for ourselves. That's the message we Christmas Pilgrims are invited to hear and receive.

When we feel unloved and unwanted, it's very important to remember that a Savior has been born. Sometimes perhaps you feel like borrowing a line from this baby's ancestor David and cry out, "No one cares for my life!" But the message to the shepherds and to you is, "I care. I care enough to send my Son to die for you." The message conveyed by angels is a message of love, from a God who cares for you.

It's significant that what the shepherds saw and heard that night in Bethlehem produced worship in their hearts. They went back to the fields glorifying and praising God for all the things they had heard and seen. I wonder if there's a clue here about why we may sometimes have a hollow, boring experience when we go to worship. When we fail to appreciate what God has done for us, we are not likely to worship him. Worship flows from grateful hearts. When we see and hear what God is doing, our natural response should be awe-filled thanksgiving. Maybe we've lost sight of the wonder of Jesus and the awesome power of God.

The message of the angels to the shepherds is also a message of assurance. God keeps every promise he makes. The promises and prophecies had been stacking up for centuries. Israel's faithlessness and rebellion had brought hard times to the chosen people. Did it seem that God had forsaken them and that his promises were empty? The birth of Jesus in Bethlehem was a startling and convincing reminder to the remnant of Israel that God keeps every promise.

The story about the shepherds ends with Luke saying that what they saw and heard when they went to see Jesus was just as they had been told. The disciples would learn later that whatever Jesus told them was going to happen would in fact happen just like he said. There's a lot of doubt and confusion about truth these days. Wouldn't it be good if we could have confidence in the middle of so much uncertainty? We're not sure who we can believe when some politicians and advertisers make ridiculous promises that insult our intelligence. Maybe you've been hurt by lies from people you trusted and you've grown a hard shell of skepticism and doubt in self-defense. I pray that God will grant you and me grace to believe what he tells us. I am confident that, not only on this journey to

Bethlehem, but on all our journeys, we will find that it always turns out just as God says.

Which of the shepherds' blessings do you need most right now in your life? Does your worship need to be energized by a clear view of God? Does your confidence need a refreshing dose of assurance? Does your broken heart need a reminder that you are known and loved by God?

The

Magi

December 16

Now after Jesus was born in
Bethlehem of Judea in the days of
Herod the king, behold, wise men
from the east came to Jerusalem.
- Matthew 2:1

Melchior's mind kept racing through the star charts. What was he missing? How did it appear so suddenly? Why had no one ever charted it before?

When his part of the king's birthday ceremony ended, he rushed back to his quarters. No one asked why, at his age, he did not prefer to move to an apartment on a lower floor of the building. His joints ached with each step up the stairs, and it took a while for him to get there. But only one apartment in the complex had a balcony with an unobstructed view of the night sky.

It would be dark in two hours. Perhaps he should rest; the night ahead would be a long one. But he knew as soon as he laid his head on the pillow that sleep would not come. So moments later he was up again, poring over the drawings. His were the most prized in the kingdom, with accuracy and detail far beyond the others. But his charts did not offer a clue about the rogue.

After another night filled with wonder and frustration, he cancelled all his appointments for the day. He sent a messenger to Gaspar's apartment, calling him to a conference. He also sent word to Balthasar, using in both messages the code word that would summon his esteemed associates without question or hesitation. When the others arrived, their excitement about the business at hand made them skip the usual formalities of their meetings. Gaspar had his old scrolls. Balthasar brought the bag that held their funds.

"What did you find?" Melchior asked Gaspar, hoping that his scholarly old friend would be able to explain the odd occurrence with some reference from an obscure sacred text. Gaspar's eyes danced as he pulled out one of the oldest rolls.

"I may have something here," Gaspar said. "Look." His hands gently, masterfully unrolled the parchment, and his finger came to rest just above the passage: "A star shall rise from Jacob; a scepter out of Israel."

"What is that?" Melchior's robe flowed behind him as he strode around the table to read the old words for himself. His research partner told him that these were the words of a prophet named Balaam. Although the prediction was contained in Hebrew Scriptures, Balaam was not one of the Hebrew God's prophets, but rather a Gentile, employed by Balak, king of Moab, to curse his enemy Israel. The prediction was uttered during a rather humorous incident in which Yahweh kept turning Balaam's attempts to curse Israel into blessings.

"It's from the Hebrew Scriptures. It seems to fit. If it's true, there's a new king, a different kind of king on the way," Gaspar reasoned aloud.

"Israel hasn't been a real player for centuries now," Balthasar scoffed.

"But the old stories are pretty convincing. Maybe there's something to the prophecies after all," said Gaspar.

An idea, a suggestion from beyond their own reasoning was taking shape in their minds. They walked out onto the balcony and peered into the sky. It was unmistakable. "Israel calls this coming King Messiah," Melchior said aloud. "Is the star his calling card? Has the promised one arrived?" Melchior and Gaspar looked to Balthasar, their treasurer.

"The journey will be difficult and long." Balthasar was telling them what they already knew. "The proper gifts alone will cost a fortune." He realized that his analysis was not going to stop this idea. The star's bright beam beckoned them. Its magnetism drew them. The seekers were about to hit the road.

No one really knows who the wise men were, or exactly where they came from. Who do you imagine they were?

(Note: I am grateful for Michael Card's book *The Promise*, for its influence on my thinking about the Magi.)

December 17

"Where is he who has been born
king of the Jews? For we saw his star
when it rose and have come to
worship him." - Matthew 2:2

As mysterious as the name by which we know them, the *Magi* (or wise men) were Christmas Pilgrims, too. A journalism student, taught to ask who, what, when, where, why and how, would probably find it difficult to write a lead paragraph, much less an entire story about these people who came to Bethlehem to see a newborn king.

All the details from Scripture about the Magi are in the first 12 verses of Matthew chapter two. Everything else about them is from legend, tradition and speculation. Some sources tell their names—Melchior, Gaspar and Balthasar. Others tell us they were Persian astronomer-astrologers. Maybe the number of gifts suggests there were three wise men, but we really don't know.

Matthew tells us the *when*—when Jesus was born in the days of Herod the king. We also know the *where*—the destination of their pilgrimage, even if we're unsure of their starting point. They were guided by a star to the vicinity and then to the exact location where they found Jesus. We know the *why* in their own words: "We have come to worship the King of the Jews." The *how* question is partially answered. They bowed down and presented gifts. But how did they know?

The writer of Hebrews in the New Testament began his book by saying that God spoke at many times and in varying ways. He communicated through prophets' inspired words and dramatic actions, through a hand that wrote mysteriously on a wall, even once through a talking donkey. And at least once through a mysterious star, God sent words of instruction and invitation to seekers.

The writer of Hebrews also said that in these last days, God has spoken to us by his Son. All those methods and messengers from God in the Old Testament were pointing to the one through whom we hear from God today—Jesus. Do you remember the story about Jesus' transfiguration? Peter, James and John saw Jesus talking with Moses and Elijah. Then they heard the voice of God saying, "This is my beloved Son, with whom I am well pleased; listen to him." We listen to the one the wise men followed the star to find.

These Christmas Pilgrims are well-known from nativity scenes and Christmas pageants. Every self-respecting nativity set has wise men in it, whether it's made of life-sized plastic figures for the yard or delicate, hand-painted porcelain for the coffee table. It's ironic that some of the best known characters in the manger scene were probably not even there. The wise men came later, maybe as much as two years later, according to the incidents reported by Matthew. But they did come. They came a long way, brought costly gifts and bowed down to worship King Jesus.

Their deep knowledge of ancient mysteries and their probable position as advisors to powerful kings could have filled the wise men with so much pride that such a journey and such behavior would have been unthinkable. But somehow God got their attention. Pride and position were cast aside, and they came in humility to worship the promised one.

Michael B. McElroy

Knowledge can be a bridge to worship for some people, but for others a barrier to worship. How is that possible? Which is it in your heart? What makes the difference?

64

December 18

"I see him, but not now; I behold
him, but not near: a star shall come
out of Jacob, and a scepter shall rise
out of Israel;" - Numbers 24:17

It's interesting that God used a visible sign (the rogue star) and a centuries-old prophecy (from a rogue prophet) to call these pilgrims to Bethlehem. Old Balaam is mentioned in five Old Testament books and three times in the New Testament, but never in a positive light. How odd that his words would be the ones that called them across the miles and centuries: "I see him, but not now; I behold him, but not near. A star will come out of Jacob; a scepter will rise out of Israel."

This reminds us that God comes to us and calls us where we are. That is of course ultimately true in Jesus coming into the world to become like us to save us. We hear it when Jesus tells fishermen that he will make them fishers of men. What better way to reach these scholars of ancient religion and astronomy than to tie an old writing to a new star?

God's willingness to do that is amazing to me. But the wise men's willingness to give up on incantation and knowledge and to follow the star is amazing and instructive, too. They were willing to follow the light they had (quite literally), and it led them to worship King Jesus. That explains why these Gentiles from who knows where came a long way to Bethlehem to worship, while the Jewish religious leaders just down the road in Jerusalem did not.

I would never discount what you know in urging you to make this pilgrimage. I don't know how God might use your background and experience to draw you to himself, but I do not doubt that he will do it. The issue is willingness. Are we willing to listen? Are we willing to follow? Are we willing to humble ourselves, and be genuine seekers?

Pilgrim, are you a long way from acknowledging Jesus as King in your life and heart? Will it cost you a lot to do so? Will it mean that you have to give up things you've long known and practiced? My prayer about this is that God will grant us the grace to remember these pilgrims who followed the star, and walk in their steps. We don't call them "wise men" for nothing.

The Magi followed the "light" they had—the star. Would you have followed such a sign? Are you content to follow the "light" you have—the Bible?

Herod

December 19

When Herod the king heard this,
he was troubled, and all Jerusalem
with him. - Matthew 2:3

Not everyone was filled with joy when news of Jesus' birth began to circulate. The shepherds rejoiced when they heard the news of a newborn Savior. But King Herod was troubled when he heard from the wise men about a baby who had been born whom they described as "king of the Jews." Instead of elation and relief, Herod felt threatened and angry.

History tells us that the Herods were ruthless despots. Although they were vassals, really no more than hand puppets who served at the pleasure and for the convenience of Rome, they fiercely protected their turf. That may be why Herod was troubled. It certainly explains the murder of all the little boys less than two years old. The Herods killed their own family members if those brothers or children were perceived to be threats. They would not hesitate to slaughter innocent children for the same reason.

Rather than just shaking our heads at the cruelty, let's take a closer look at why Herod was troubled to make sure our own reaction to the good news about Jesus is altogether joyful. You see, Herod probably reacted as he did because he felt the newborn King was a threat to his own throne and crown. You and I know from reading the rest of the story that Jesus' kingdom would not be of this world. It would not be a political, territorial entity, but an all-encompassing spiritual kingdom. But Herod didn't know that. The popular idea about Messiah was that he would restore David's throne and throw off the evil oppressors of the Jews. Even the closest disciples fantasized about their places in the glorious new kingdom. When Herod heard the word "king," he felt threatened. Do you?

Jesus described his control of the hearts, minds and lives of his disciples as "the kingdom of God." Jesus is Lord as well as Savior, and those who follow him must deny themselves to do so. That means we give up on being our own king, and bow down to Jesus as ruler of our lives. It is precisely here that many of us balk. Church is fine, and we realize that we are actually blessed when people around us do what Jesus wants them to do. But we feel threatened when our will is challenged by his will. It is not easy to pray what Jesus prayed in Gethsemane: "Not my will, but yours be done."

It breaks my heart to realize that I have the potential within me to resist and reject the kingship of Jesus just as Herod did. But it's true. Every act of willful disobedience to God in our lives demonstrates to some degree the resistance that Herod felt. You know what I mean, Pilgrim?

We worship Jesus as King. We sing songs about his crown, his throne, his kingdom. How do our daily lives and moment-to-moment decisions test our worship?

December 20

And he sent them to Bethlehem,
saying, "Go and search diligently for
the child, and when you have found
him, bring me word, that I too may
come and worship him."
- Matthew 2:8

Herod told the wise men to tell him when they found Jesus so that he too could "come and worship" the baby king. Is our worship tainted with a similar hypocrisy when we sing about Jesus being King while clinging to the illusion that we control our own lives? We may say Amen to the prayers at church that praise God as the great King of the universe. But do we at other times stake our claim on the Judea of our hearts and defy his rightful reign over us? Are these uncomfortable questions? I do not mean to be insulting. But these are questions we may need to ask ourselves.

As Christmas Pilgrims, we have a decision to make. We dare not go to Bethlehem as mere curiosity-seekers. We shouldn't be making the journey simply because it is seasonally or culturally expedient to do so. We cannot go to the manger and treat the baby we find there as if he were an offering at a cafeteria: "Oh, the Savior is really appealing. I'll take that, but I think I'll pass on that Lordship." And we must admit that it is possible to go on the journey, to go through the motions, and it all be a sham—no more real than Herod's pretense of worship.

Remember that the Herods were not really kings, not really in control, but simply instruments of Roman imperialism. Ironically, the Herods weren't really Jews either. They were Idumeans, installed on the throne at Jerusalem by the Romans. Old Herod was altogether an imposter as king of the Jews. And Pilgrim, you and I are imposters when we think we're in control! The territory of our hearts is not rightfully ours; we're not actually in control.

The wise men's gifts were expensive, truly fit for a king. But the greatest gifts we could bring to King Jesus are our unconditional surrender of self and genuine worship from our heart. Those precious commodities cost us more than gold, frankincense and myrrh. Giving ourselves to Jesus is an extravagant gift, since it takes all we have and all we are to truly give it. And isn't it wonderful that the only thing we really have to give that we can call our own is exactly what honors Jesus most when we give it to him?

Think about "Your kingdom come, Your will be done" from the Lord's Prayer. Focus on your own heart and life as you pray those words.

Jesus

December 21

And at the end of eight days, when
he was circumcised, he was called
Jesus, the name given by the angel
before he was conceived in the womb.
- Luke 2:21

Somewhere in our stuff, probably in a box of old photographs, there is a page of names that we considered before our first child was born. It was 1982, over a year before I would buy my first real computer, so the list is typewritten. I remember the night we sat in my basement office and said the names aloud. I typed a dozen or more possibilities, both boy's names and girl's names. (It was 1982. We didn't know in advance the sex of our firstborn.) Even when she was born, we were still undecided about her full name until she was about three days old. We stared at the blank for the name on the birth certificate a couple of days before committing. But when we came home from the hospital, she was Heather Suzanne McElroy.

Mary knew her baby would be a boy and knew his name would be Jesus before she was even pregnant. She had no pregnancy test, 4-D ultrasound image or baby name book. But she knew because the angel said so. When Joseph came and reported the collaborating message he received from the angel, she knew. Later, after the baby had been born, the delay until the eighth day was a formality of the Jewish circumcision ritual, not the inability of young parents to make a choice about something as important as a child's name.

He was called by more than one name in the prophecies—Wonderful Counselor, Mighty God, Everlasting Father, Prince of Peace, Immanuel to name a few. Each emphasized some aspect of his character, nature or mission. But when the angel told Joseph the name that would be spoken when it was time for ancient Israel's equivalent of the birth certificate, that name was Jesus.

Do you know the meaning of your name? Do you know the story of how your parents chose your name? Does it have some family significance?

December 22

*"She will bear a son, and you
shall call his name Jesus, for he will
save his people from their sins."*
- Matthew 1:21

When the baby born at Bethlehem was named Jesus, the shadow of the cross was in that name. Although Yeshua was a common name among the Jews, this savior would be the Savior in the ultimate sense of the word. He would save his people out of a fallen world from the guilt, dominion and punishment of sin. He would lay down his life so his saved ones could live without fear of death. He is the Christ, God's anointed. He is Lord of all, and all will confess that truth someday whether we've done so in this world or not. But grateful hearts who know him as Savior love to praise him by his given name—Jesus.

I understand how the baby in the manger that we Christmas Pilgrims long to see may be more appealing than the gruesome execution scene of the man on the cross. But the manger is the necessary prelude to the cross. The One who would die for human beings had to take our form and nature to do so. And the cross was the necessary conclusion of the manger story if God's plan for redeeming us was to be realized. The guilt of sin required a death. We are glad to know that Immanuel (God with us) was born. That message gives us hope. By his life and words, we gain wisdom and guidance for our lives. We can do better than we've done by listening to him and imitating him. The birth of Jesus gives us joy and hope. But it's his death that deals with our sins.

Jesus accepted our punishment in our place. Those who trust in his death and believe in his resurrection can know why they named him Jesus, Savior.

The angels were predicting the cross when they told Mary and Joseph to name the baby Jesus. When the angels told the shepherds that a Savior had been born, they were predicting the cross more than thirty years in advance. On our way to Bethlehem, we must mix our joy at his birth with the somber realization that his name looks ahead to his death. Many Jews died on crosses in the time of Jesus. But only one was the Savior, born to die for you and me.

The manger and the cross are like bookends on the story of Jesus' life in flesh. Take a while to think about what his birth and his death mean to you. Take a moment and thank him for dying on the cross for you.

December 23

And when the time came for their
purification according to the Law of
Moses, the brought him up to
Jerusalem, to present him to the
Lord... - Luke 2:22

Our pilgrimage to Bethlehem now takes a side trip. Just 41 days after Jesus' birth and six miles up the road from the little town where he was born, we find baby Jesus, Mary and Joseph at the temple in Jerusalem. Luke's description gives more evidence of how deeply devout Mary and Joseph were.

The young parents were following the ancient instructions about the redemption of the firstborn and the ritual of purification following childbirth. In the shadow of the first Passover on the eve of the Exodus from Egypt, God told Moses that all the firstborn among the people and animals of Israel belonged to Him. He later exchanged the 22,000 Levites for the 22,273 firstborn counted in the census ordered a little over a year after the Exodus. Each of the firstborn in excess of the number of the Levites would be redeemed for the price of five shekels (about two ounces) of silver. All the faithful of Israel through the generations observed this custom. Luke does not mention the coins, but does tell us that "they went to Jerusalem to present him to the Lord," an echo of the texts that called for the redemption of the firstborn.

Does Luke also quietly inform us of the young couple's economic status? Back in Leviticus, the Lord told the Israelites to bring a lamb for a burnt offering and a pigeon or turtledove for a sin offering for the atonement ceremony. But if the family could not afford a lamb, two birds would be acceptable. Is Luke saying Mary and Joseph were poor when they brought a pair of turtledoves? Later in life, Jesus frankly told professing followers that he had no home of his own. He looked for breakfast on fig trees and had only one garment to his name at the time of his death.

In a world that measures greatness and significance by dollars and possessions, Jesus does not seem to measure up. This is a lesson I need to hear as Christmas approaches. We think about spending enough, giving enough and maybe even getting enough. We buy and give and get and accumulate, all in the name of the one who said that life does not consist in the abundance of possessions. I do not want to dampen your holiday spirit. But I need to be reminded (and maybe you do, too) that Jesus came and did without what this world thinks is valuable. And he did it for us. A half-century after the events described by Luke, Paul would use Jesus' poverty to motivate generosity among his disciples: "For you know the grace of our Lord Jesus Christ, that though he was rich, yet for your sake he became poor, so that you by his poverty might become rich."

We admire Mary and Joseph's devotion to the Law and its customs. We're thankful to know that the boy Jesus grew up in a family that respected the word of God. But surely there is more for us to see in this report of their obedience. I think it's significant that the baby at the center of this picture is the one who came because the whole nation (not just the firstborn) needed to be redeemed, and not just the nation, but also the whole fallen race. The human family needed a purification that could be foreshadowed, but not accomplished by the sacrifice of animals. "It is impossible for the blood of bulls and goats to take away sins." As part of his identification with us, our Lord himself became a baby to be redeemed, born of a mother with whom he went through the purification ritual. And then, when he went to the cross, he himself became the redemption price. His blood became the real and effective purifying sacrifice for our sins. We Christmas Pilgrims find yet another reason to bow down and worship. It's not only about how far Jesus came. It's also about how far he would go.

Can you think of a way to remind yourself and your family that Christmas is about much more than the gifts that are exchanged?

Please pause and meditate for a while about the wonder of Jesus humbling himself to become a baby, going through the ritual of redemption and purification, and then ultimately becoming the sacrifice to redeem and purify you.

December 24

*And she gave birth to her firstborn
son and wrapped him in swaddling
cloths and laid him in a manger,
because there was no place for them
in the inn. - Luke 2:7*

We never took long vacations when I was a boy. My
father worked hard, long hours every day. But we would
sometimes go to the Gulf Coast for two or three days
during the summer.

Back then, we never had reservations in advance. Part
of the vacation ritual was going from motel to motel,
looking for a room in a place that would be acceptable.
In my mind, more than fifty years later, I can still see the
signs in front of the motels. The word "Vacancy" was
painted on the sign, just like the name of the place. The
signs might have white or blue or green neon tubing
outlining the letters. But the word "NO" was in red neon.
The proprietor could switch it on or off depending on
how many customers had signed the register that day, or
whether or not the person getting out of the car looked
like a desirable guest. The sun was going down. I wanted
to be on the beach, not riding up and down the road after
being in the car all day. I hated the cruel, red "NO" that
told me I was not welcome.

Luke explains in one simple line why Jesus was laid
in a manger: "because there was no place for them in the
inn." Like hotels in college towns on home game

weekends, or motels from a simpler time along the beach, Bethlehem's inns were packed, filled with travelers who had come to comply with Rome's decree to register. When Mary and Joseph arrived, they could not find shelter in the inn.

Forget Ramada or Holiday. This inn from Jesus' day was probably not more than a group of open sheds surrounding a common area. I won't describe it as a courtyard because that's probably too dignified a term for it, and it might make you think of yet another modern hotel chain. Forget quaint, charming, cozy and all the other advertising words that describe today's "homes away from home." In reality, the inn itself was probably not as nice as the stables we see in the annual dramas commemorating Jesus' birth. It would get zero stars in the hotel rating guides.

There's a character called the Innkeeper in most Christmas plays, but we don't find one in the gospel narrative. We don't know if Mary and Joseph were rudely turned away by the proprietor, or angrily driven out of the crowded space by the other guests. Maybe they just peeked in the gate, hoping for a corner in the corral where Mary could rest, before realizing that there was no room.

So Mary and Joseph had to improvise. Was Jesus born in a cave under the inn, or in a stable where the animals were kept? Or was he born in the open air? We don't know. What we do know is that there was no room in the inn for newborn Jesus.

What emotions are stirred in you when you read there was no room for Mary and Joseph, and that Jesus' first bassinet was an animal feeding trough? What does Luke's account of this have to do with your life?

You

December 25

He came to his own, and his own
people did not receive him. But to all
who did receive him, who believed in
his name, he gave the right to become
children of God, who were born, not
of blood nor of the will of the flesh
nor of the will of man, but of God.
And the Word became flesh and dwelt
among us, and we have seen his
glory, glory as of the only Son from
the Father, full of grace and truth.
- John 1:11-14

Pilgrim, you're probably ahead of me on this one,
aren't you? You know what I'm going to ask. Do you,
my fellow Christmas Pilgrim, have room in your heart
and in your life for Jesus? We think it's sad that the
Savior of the world had to be born in such a difficult
situation. We shake our heads as we imagine the poverty
in which he lived his life, remembering how he warned
a prospective disciple, "Foxes have holes, and birds of
the air have nests, but the Son of Man has nowhere to lay
his head." And the lack of accommodation he found in
his birth and life was mirrored in the hard-hearted
rejection he experienced from the very people he came
to save. "He came to his own, and his own people did not
receive him."

But do we have room for him in our crowded lives?
The innkeeper and other guests could not have known

they were turning away the Messiah. Maybe you're like them, and just didn't know. But I know. Maybe you do, too. We know and believe he is "the only Son from the Father, full of grace and truth." Do we still sometimes find no room for Jesus in the inn of our hearts? Our preoccupation with our plans and desires, our ongoing need to acquire more stuff, and the incessant demands of business and family life make it hard for Jesus to find a place, let alone first place in far too many lives.

You might be like my friend, a young, hard-working businessman. He was not making excuses when he told me that he simply did not have time to read his Bible and pray. I didn't have to tell him how important it was. He knew he should. But from the time he was awakened by the clock in the early morning until he collapsed from exhaustion late in the evening, it was hard to find room in his day for time with God. Is your day like that? Others have so many things that need to be done every day, or so many activities planned that they simply cannot find room for God.

As Christmas Pilgrims, let's commit to make room for Jesus. We've read this book and thought these thoughts on a purposeful, thirty-day journey together to see Jesus during the Christmas season. We've made it to Christmas. That's good. I commend you for doing it. The real challenge is to make real room for Christ tomorrow, and in the real routine of our daily lives.

Most of us live with very little margin. If one part of our plan doesn't happen on time, our tightly scheduled events can topple like falling dominoes. Media outlets constantly inundate us, each clamoring for our attention. We're driven by the desire to acquire. It's hard to concentrate, to carve out time, to make room. It's not always easy to obey, "Be still and know that I am God." But it is important. Taking time to read, think and pray in quietness every day is one of the most important and rewarding commitments a disciple of Jesus can make.

So, it's a day for gift-giving. I believe the most important gift you could give today would be the gift of yourself to the Lord. We owe him far more than just a little time each day or week. I'm talking about surrendering your whole life to Jesus, who came so far to live and die and rise again for you.

Thank you for reading, for sharing this journey with me. Merry Christmas, Pilgrim. I pray that God's inexpressible gift, the gift of his Son, will be yours this Christmas Day, and every day. God bless you!

What comes to your mind when you read the apostle Paul's words calling Jesus God's "inexpressible gift"?

If it's difficult to schedule daily time for Bible reading and prayer in your routine, think of one change you could make that would create some time. Could you implement that change tomorrow? Will you do it? Please say YES, Pilgrim! Then by God's grace stay on the journey with Jesus until you arrive at Home!

Afterword

Thank you for reading *Christmas Pilgrims—A Journey to Bethlehem.* I'm honored that you spent some time during the busy Christmas season with me on our pilgrimage to Bethlehem. I pray that God has used this little book to bless you.

Thanks to my team of Beta readers for their input and reactions to this book. They made *Christmas Pilgrims* better by pointing out needed corrections and clarifications. I am indebted to them all for their assistance. Special thanks to my mentor and friend Walter Albritton, without whose encouragement and guidance this book would not have been finished. Thanks for being "in my balcony," Walter.

If this book has been helpful to you, would you consider doing a couple of things now that our journey is completed? Would you please take a few minutes to leave a review of *Christmas Pilgrims* on Amazon.com? Reviews are important to help reach more people with a book's message. To write a review, go to amazon.com. In the search box, enter Christmas Pilgrims, and on the product page, click on Reviews under the author's name. Then click on Write a Review. Fill in the review page form and click Submit. Also, please recommend my books to your friends. I'd be very grateful.

If you enjoyed Christmas Pilgrims, you might also enjoy *The Abiding Companion—A Friendly Guide for Your Journey Through the New Testament.* This much larger book offers insight and practical application with an essay written for each of the New Testament's 260 chapters. It is not a commentary, but a daily companion reader. *The Abiding Companion* is also available from Amazon.com.

If you would like signed copies of either or both books, just email me for details. I'd love to hear your reactions to the books as well. My email address is mbmcelroy@gmail.com.

www.ingramcontent.com/pod-product-compliance
Lightning Source LLC
Chambersburg PA
CBHW071640050426
42443CB00026B/796